ELON MUSK Biography

For Young Readers

CONTENTS

Introduction... 1

1. The Child.. 5

2. The Reader.. 13

3. The Journey to the United States....... 21

4. The Age of the Internet.................... 31

5. PayPal.. 37

6. Aiming for Mars............................... 49

7. The Road to Liftoff.......................... 61

8. Tesla - Electrifying Personal Cars...... 69

9. Crisis... 79

10. Back from the Precipice 91

11. The Seriel Entrepreneur 99

12. The Visionary................................. 109

13. The Defender of Freedom 119

14. Words of Wisdom........................... .125

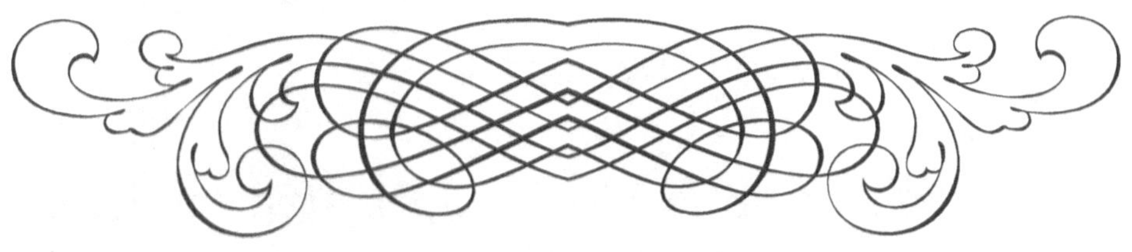

INTRODUCTION

Every now and then, there comes along someone who represents the best of their generation and leaves a huge footprint in the journey of humanity. These are the likes of Leonardo da Vinci, Albert Einstein, Marie Curie, Thomas Edison, and Mother Teresa. During the course of their lives, they captivate the imagination of the entire generation and direct it to a better future. Elon Musk is definitely such person for our times.

Elon Musk is today the superstar of the

industrial world. He has companies that build bricks and companies that send electric cars into deep space using his own roaring rockets. But he is not like the industrialists of the past era who exploited wealth from the land or other people. He is the industrialist of the 21st century, building massive and successful companies on the foundation of technologies designed to solve problems of this world and worlds far beyond the Earth.

Today, the world is Elon's captivated audience. Every word he says and every move he makes reaches the farthest corners of the world because everything he does has a purpose far beyond himself or his companies. He is out there with everyone in his mind. If there are more Elon Musks, the world would truly be a better place. And it is for this reason that we need to study his life.

Elon's life started in South Africa as a nerdy kid of a divorced parents in a suburb where bullies reigned. From his young days, Elon dreamt of his life as that of a hero, someone with a duty to save the world. He made it a mission to help humanity. And he was not going to do it if he stayed in South Africa, a country tortured by a brutal apartheid regime.

Elon made his way to Canada using his mother's citizenship and then landed in his final destination: US of A. In the entire world, this was the only country where he could realize his dreams and create technologies equivalent to magic, the kind that draws thousands to watch a Falcon Heavy take off. But should we idolize someone for only what they do and did? No.

We can't do exactly like Steve Jobs and expect to be a visionary like him. And we can't copy Mozart and expect to be the next Mozart. When we study heroes, we look at the blueprint of their thoughts and actions. This blueprint is what we should be after.

In this book you will find the template of Elon Musk that you can apply to your life, most importantly his way of looking at life and the world and the way he sees his own role in it. We can't copy actions – so many things have changed to make it worth the effort and make a difference. But we can copy the thoughts and apply them in our context and achieve astounding results. We need to think like our heroes; not act like them.

And just like all heroes, Elon is not a flawless human. He got his own deficiencies. Afterall he is just a human like everyone else. But a scientist would not focus all her effort on the speck on her microscope. Doing so will hide the grander picture that can be seen through the unobstructed parts of the lens. Similarly, we need to look at Elon not for his flaws but for his achievements, already too many to count. In looking at his life, we find a rich trove of lessons we can use in our own lives.

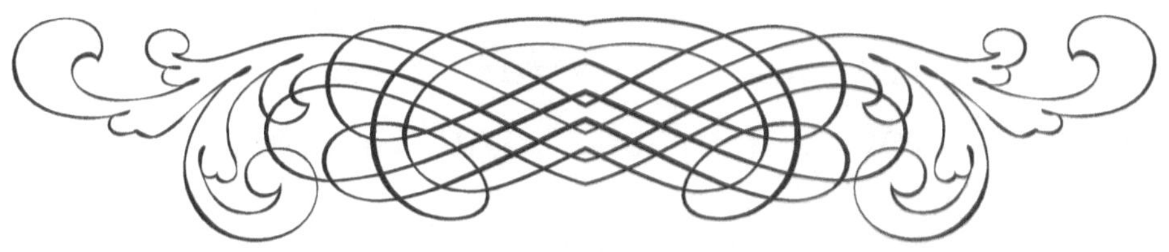

I. THE CHILD

Elon Reeve Musk was born on June 28, 1971 in Pretoria, South Africa. South Africa is one of the largest countries in Africa and Pretoria is one of its three capital cities.

Elon's parents were wealthy white South Africans. His mother is Maye Musk. She is a successful model and a dietitian. Even though she was born in Canada, she was raised in South Africa. Her father, who was American from Minnesota, was a pilot who loved adventures. He was the first person to fly from

South Africa to Australia on a single engine airplane that had no electronics or modern navigation system to guide his flight route.

Elon's father is Errol Musk, an electrotechnical engineer, pilot, sailor and a property developer. At one time, he also part-owned an emerald mine in the country of Zambia. Elon is the eldest of the three children from his parents. He has a younger brother and a sister.

With the family's wealth, Elon and his family could afford to live in a suburb of Pretoria where mostly wealthy white people lived. The family would travel out of Africa frequently, which was a luxury few South Africans could afford at that time. Elon remembers going to Paris when he was six years old and since then it has been one of his favorite cities. When the family went on these travels, the children would sometimes take emeralds in their pockets to sell if they needed money. So, growing up, money was never a problem for Elon.

Despite the wealth and privilege, Elon did not have a happy childhood. At the time of his birth, South Africa had a huge problem. The small population of white people ruled the majority native South Africans through a system called apartheid. This system denied non-white South Africans the basic rights such as education, housing, and vote while the white South Africans enjoyed everything. A black South African, for instance, was not allowed to go to beaches that were reserved for white South Africans. Naturally, South Africa was a violent and an unequal country. As a child, Elon was not spared this violence in the country.

In his childhood, Elon was bullied severely. He was a bit of a misfit in a society that valued masculinity and aggression. He was one of the youngest and smallest students in his class and also one of the smartest students in the school which made Elon an easy target for bullies. He would get beat up. One time, his bullies beat him up till he became unconscious. He had to be hospitalized.

However, not going to school because of bullies was not an option. In school, he would hide in his classroom during recess to avoid crossing paths with bullies. Outside the classroom, he would simply run and escape from them. In his childhood, Elon changed six schools because the family moved around a lot. This did not help Elon with making friends or being free from school bullies. School was a torture and Elon hated it.

Elon did not and still does not agree with the way schools educate children. Children are all put in a classroom and taught all subjects without any consideration for the children's preferences or interests. Schools act like factory: children enter school where they are made to learn all sorts of thing and then after going from one grade to the next, they come out at the other end. He thinks children should be allowed to progress at the fastest pace they are capable of going rather than staying in one grade for an entire year.

But Elon had some good memories from his primary school, Waterkloof House Preparatory School. There he came across his best teacher ever: the school principal. The principal had to substitute after their math teacher quit. The students had to really rush and work hard to catch up on the math syllabus. To encourage students to work hard, the principal would tell fascinating stories of World War II during which he was a solder but only after the students had done their work. All children worked hard. This principal left a lasting impression on Elon who believe learning can be made interesting so that children do not feel like it is a chore.

When Elon was nine, his parents divorced. He initially lived with his mother but feeling sorry for his father, he and his brother Kimbal chose to live with their father. Elon really did not like his father and their relation still remain estranged.

Even during his childhood, Elon was very driven. Once he set his goal, he would go for it. One time when he was six years old, he was grounded by his parents and stopped from going to a cousin's birthday party. He was left at home when his parents and siblings went to the party. But Elon felt it was unfair and he was determined to go to the party.

He escaped from his nanny and started

walking toward his cousin's house. The only problem was his cousin lived 12 miles away. And he did not really know the way from his house to his cousin's house. But he managed to reach his destination after four hours of walking. It was a stupid thing for the young Elon to do: He could have got hit by a car or kidnapped on the road. But it shows his determination and stubbornness even as a child.

Like that of many, Elon Musk's childhood was full of contradictions: privileged but a minority, smart but a victim of bully, peaceful home in a violent nation. It was definitely not a smooth sailing. But Elon never allowed any of those challenges to derail him from his true path. If any, those challenges hardened him, and gave him the capacity to take pain and that "never give up" attitude that he is known for.

Today, Elon runs multiple, high-value companies, while also working as the chief engineer and marketer at the same time for his companies. He truly appears to have a superior brain and inherent intelligence. But this is not entirely true. All average humans are born with potentials. Elon is someone who has achieved his high potentials. Not because of his inherent talents but through discipline, inquisitive effort and hard work that he put into learning and developing an attitude of steel from his childhood until now. School was rough for Elon, but that was not excuse for not coming to school in neat and tidy clothes, as his geography teacher recalled. Elon is not a proof of inbuilt talent; he is a proof of what humans are capable of achieving with enough focus, drive and effort.

fact

When Elon was a child, he would often go into deep thought. In this mode, he would not hear anyone and would stay wherever he was with a distant look in his eyes. This happened so often that Elon's parents and doctor thought he was deaf. They decided to remove his adenoid glands to improve his hearing. This, however, did not change anything in Elon. They did not know that even from very young days, Elon was a deep thinker. And when he entered into a trance-like state, he was simply in a deep thought.

Elon says that his mind works in a very visual way. He is able to think with high clarity. When his mind finds something interesting to work on, he would imagine every component and see in his mind's eyes how each component behaved and interacted. When his mind was engaged in such thought experiments, he would block out the world and dedicate all his concentration to a single task.

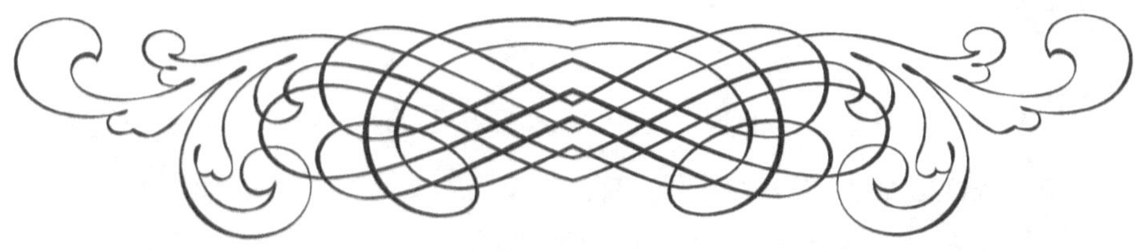

II. THE READER

"Not all readers are leaders, but all leaders are readers" – Harry S Truman

From a very young age, Elon Musk was a voracious reader of books. By age six, he was reading books. Not that he was born a reader but there was nothing else to do. And he got bored easily. He always had to do something to stay engaged and TV was not helpful. It had only one channel and it was on only for half a day. His boredom forced him to read a lot.

Elon would read anything. He read any comics he could get his hands on: Superman, Batman, Green Lantern, Iron Man. When he couldn't find any comics around, he would sneak into the bookstores and read there until he was chased away. At school, dodging bullies had one advantage. It gave Elon plenty of time for him to be alone with books.

His love for reading was far greater than the books available to him. By the age of 9, he had finished reading all there was to read. In desperation, he turned to reading the entire set of encyclopedias. Encyclopedias are thick volumes of book that contain all facts about the world. Before there was the Internet, encyclopedia was the Google: If you wanted to learn a fact, you would turn to them.

Elon's love for reading, which continues to the day, is one reason he can learn any subject very fast. Reading, after all, is a far more efficient way of transferring information into your brain. Reading also taught Elon to search for truth. Not just any truth, but scientific truth. Whenever he came across something, one of the first questions he asked was: is this true?

His search for truth even saved him from his fear of the dark. Through books and his scientific mind, he came to know that darkness really only means the absence of photons in the visible wavelength. He thought it was silly of him to be afraid of dark because all it really meant was the absence of some photons. Since then, he was never afraid of the dark.

His reading made him ask questions on all sorts of things. The questions then forced him to search for answers. He would pester his parents with a never-ending stream of questions to the point of annoying them. And sometimes, his bookish knowledge would irritate his friends. For example, one day he heard someone say that the distance between moon is 250,000 kilometers. Elon corrected promptly: 384,400 kilometers.

As he grew up, he read thousands of books. He read fictions such as The Lord of the Rings and The Hobbit by JRR Tolkien. But the books he found most interesting was sci-fi. One of his most favorite books remain The Hitchhiker's Guide to Galaxy by Douglas Adams.

It is obvious that books had the most influence in shaping the most prolific and impactful entrepreneur of the 21st century. Reading provided Elon an escape from, sometimes, the hell he was going through, and the mundane and the dramatic events of the day. It forced him to ask the most fundamental questions about his life and its purpose. He found that his life, like any other lives, has no inherent purpose but he can make it a purposeful one for himself. But what would that be? Here again, books showed him the way. He wanted to develop technologies to solve the biggest problems facing humanity. One question he asked after reading The Hitchhiker's Guide to the Galaxy was, what would happen if the planet Earth was, for instance struck by a giant asteroid that would wipe all life forms from the face of the planet? We have no other planets to go to. Elon then resolved to make human a multi-planetary species, capable of going and colonizing other planets. Mars is his first destination.

In addition to reading, Elon was very fond of video games. This again was in the pre-

Internet period. There were no online video games. Far from it. Video games, with extremely poor graphics by today's standards, came in small consoles.

When he got his first computer at the age of 10, he spent many nights and days obsessively learning to code. He took some computer classes but found them useless. He was far ahead of his teachers. Elon got himself a book on computer programing which was supposed to take a user six months. He mastered it in three days.

While reading books from a young age certainly helped Elon become what he is today, he wished he had not read some of those books at such an age. He made the mistake of reading books by German philosophers Nietzsche and Arthur Schopenhauer. They were negative and depressive and he regretted reading them at a young age. The things he learnt from religious and philosophical books actually made it quite traumatic for Elon as he battled with questions about the meaning of life.

While there is no age too young to start

reading, it is better to be mindful of what kind of books you read. In younger days, it is better to pick books that expand your imaginative power, the things that make you wonder about the world and the universe we live in. Good science fictions are something you should read in your younger days.

The science fictions Elon read intrigued him on the technological possibilities to create "magic", to do what seems otherwise impossible. Elon decided that he would use his life to invent and create things.

"The heroes of the books I read always felt a duty to save the world" – Elon Musk

Eight favorite Books of Elon Musk:
1. The Lord of the Rings and The Hobbit by JRR Tolkien
2. The Hitchhiker's Guide to the Galaxy by Douglas Adams
3. Benjamin Franklin: An American Life by Walter Isaacson
4. Einstein: His Life and Universe by Walter Isaacson

5.   Superintelligence: Paths, Dangers, Strategies by Nick Bostrom
6.   Lord of the Flies by William Golding
7.   The Foundation Trilogy by Isaac Asimov
8.   Structures: Or Why Things Don't Fall Down by J.E. Gordon

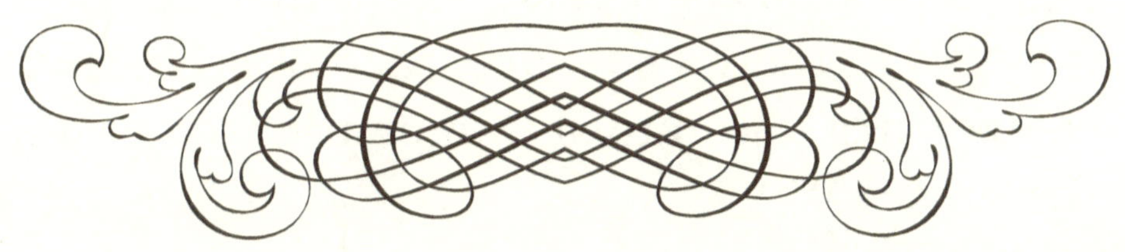

III. THE JOURNEY TO THE UNITED STATES

When we look at Elon's life with all his successes, we think that he always knew what he wanted to do in life. That was not the case. In his younger days, he did not know what to do with his life, and not knowing was painful for him. But unlike most young people, he thought a lot about what he wanted to do.

By age 14 or 15, Elon had some idea of what he wanted to do with his life. He wanted to create technologies to solve problems and build things on an inter-planetary scale. For this, he needed latest technologies and technologies that do not yet exist. One thing was certain: there was no way he would solve problems and build things if he stayed in South Africa. In terms of technology, South Africa was not the most happening place on Earth. Most importantly, if he stayed, there was only one road ahead, leading straight into a cantonment of South African army.

Under the apartheid South Africa, white boys were required by the law to join the military. Once conscripted, they were expected to perform military services whenever called for by the government. Compulsory conscription was coming Elon's way as he neared the age of 16, the age of conscription. Elon dreaded joining the army, whose sole function was to oppress non-white South Africans. A huge political storm was also brewing in South Africa, as the apartheid system reached the end of its horrible life. It was an uncertain period and lots of white South Africans were fleeing the country.

Moving to the United States appeared to be the best option. It was the world's technology capital where all kinds of innovative technologies were created. And it had Silicon Valley. Elon imagined the technology hub to be some sort of mythical place, almost like Mount Olympus. He does not say it but one can imagine Elon dreaming of one day becoming a technology king in Silicon Valley, some sort of Zeus of this Mount Olympus. He had to go there.

How his rough childhood influenced his drive to move out of South Africa, we don't know. Yet, we can imagine that he had a strong urge to leave behind the unpleasant memories and start afresh in a faraway country.

But there was no way for him to get the US citizenship. Even though his maternal grandfather was from Minnesota, he could not use it to claim American citizenship. His only way to American citizenship was through Canada.

Elon's mother, Maye, was born in Canada which meant she and her children could get

Canadian passport. He pushed his mother to apply for their Canadian passport, doing all the paper works himself. When he got their Canadian passport, Elon tried to convince his parents and family to move to Canada. They refused and even tried to keep Elon from emigrating to Canada. But with conscription to the military coming his way, he had to leave South Africa in 1989. He was 17 years old.

When we now think of Elon Musk, we see a man who knows exactly what he wants and how to get what he wants. So, we naturally imagine that before he left South Africa, he would have figured out every step of the way to his final destination: Silicon Valley. But this was not the case. Elon's great escape from South Africa was not really well thought out.

Before he left home in South Africa, he was not even sure which part of Canada he would ultimately end up in. He had an uncle in Montreal, Canada. Before leaving South Africa, Elon sent a letter to his uncle informing that he was coming to Canada. He never got any reply from his uncle before he left South Africa. He hoped for the best and boarded the flight to

Canada. Upon arriving in Canada, he came to learn that his uncle had gone to Minnesota. He had come too far to return to South Africa. He spent his first night in a youth hostel. Next day, he bought a bus ticket and headed to Vancouver.

In Vancouver, he was not sure what to do. To survive, he worked odd jobs. He sold vegetables, worked at a farm and was even a lumberjack briefly, cutting logs and cleaning sawmills, the latter being particularly dangerous.

He was worried that the few thousand dollars in cash he had brought from South Africa might dry up before he could find a real job. He did an experiment to see if he could survive on one Canadian dollar a day or less on food. He found that if he bought hotdogs and buns in bulk and ate only them throughout the day, his food cost was less than a dollar. He was also afraid of scurvy. How he developed the fear of scurvy, of all diseases, is unknown, but to keep it away, he also bought oranges in bulk which he ate every couple of days. Even though his experiment was a success and he did not get scurvy, he discovered that eating hotdogs for breakfast, lunch and dinner got a little monotonous after a while.

Enrolling in college was not in his plan. But he did enroll, choosing Queen's University in Ontario, Canada. And he enrolled for college and chose Queen's not for reasons we may imagine. Elon wanted to date girls of his age and Queen's had plenty of girls. In fact, Elon met his first wife, Justine, at Queen's.

Queen's, however, gave Elon more than just his future wife. After two years at the university, he applied for scholarship to the University of Pennsylvania in the US. As ridiculous as it sounds now, Elon had no other way of paying for UPenn. Before he left South Africa, his parents made it clear that they will not fund his college studies if he went to North America.

He won the scholarship and in 1992 moved to the University of Pennsylvania, which started as Publik Academy of Philadelphia in 1749 born from the idea of one of the greatest early Americans – Benjamin Franklin. Franklin was a hero of Elon, and his life inspired Elon.

At UPenn, Elon got a double degree. He wanted to know how the economy works. So he took the Wharton finance degree. Then he wanted to figure out how the universe worked. So he studied physics. The business part of his double degree was easy. Quantum mechanics? Not so much.

As a university student, Elon did not have a lot of money. In fact, he had to find ways to earn his rent and other expenses. Perhaps as another sign of his entrepreneurial outlook, he and his roommate rented a large, ten-bedroom house which they used to host crazy parties on the weekends. In some of these parties, five hundred students would show up, paying five dollars each. Together, they would earn their rent in one weekend.

He completed his degrees in 1995. The world did not know Elon Musk yet. In fact, far from it. He was just another penniless student, faced with a choice: take a job in Wall Street and probably get a fat salary or go for PhD and solve some technical problems. He did not quite like the first option. So, he chose the second one.

Elon's Essays

As a part of his business course at UPenn, Elon was required to write a business plan. He wrote a paper on solar energy entitled "The Importance of Being Solar". The paper went on to predict a rise in solar power technology and delved deep into the workings of a solar cells and how future solar technology would work. He even depicted the power station of the future: a giant array of solar cells beaming down energy through microwave beams to a receiver on Earth. Elon received 98 for his paper.

For his physics degree, he wrote a paper on ultracapacitors and the technological progress in energy storage. Clearly, he had a fascination for everything energy. For this paper, he got 97.

US Citizenship

After Elon moved from South Africa, he got his Canadian citizenship using his mother's Canadian citizenship. His ultimate aim for US citizenship, and having Canadian citizenship made it far easier to get it then if he had remained South African.

Ten years after moving to the US, Elon took the oath of American Citizenship with 3500 other immigrants in California. His then wife, Justine, however missed the oath taking ceremony after her alarm clock malfunctioned.

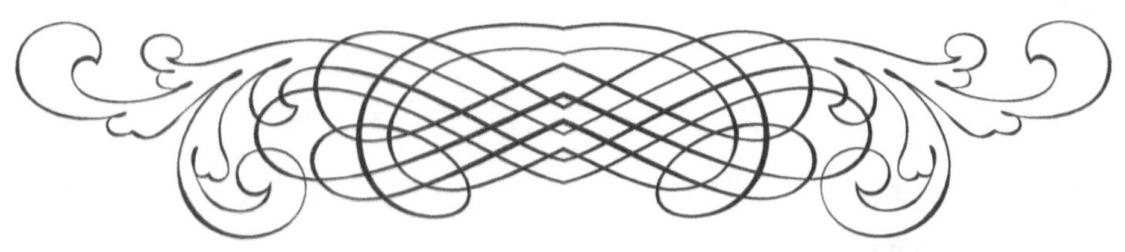

IV. THE AGE OF THE INTERNET

"The Internet is like the world acquiring a nervous system." – Elon Musk

Elon Musk today is famous for all the pathbreaking companies he started and operates. He is a serial entrepreneur of the highest order. And he had the entrepreneurial spirit in him from his childhood.

One of the first ventures he tried, even before

turning 10, was to start a video game arcade in his locality along with his younger brother and a few other friends. They drew up a business plan. They were confident it would make money because they knew what games were popular and would sell. Of course, the young entrepreneurs had their plan scraped by their parents.

Elon tasted the first fruit of his business success at the age of 12. At that time, there was a computer magazine in South Africa that brought software codes from programmers. The magazine would publish the code and pay money to the developer. Elon needed money to buy new video games. So he developed a video game called Blaster and sold the code to the magazine. It was the first product ever developed by Elon. He received several hundred dollars for the code. He was 12 years at the time which, more than anything, shows that you are never too young to start inventing and building stuffs.

After Elon got his double degrees from UPenn, he decided to do PhD at Stanford University. But he dropped out two days later. He saw an opportunity too good to miss.

In 1995, the Internet was going through a rapid growth phase. It was the talk of the town, and indeed of the world. What was earlier reserved only for the American military and some universities was becoming a part of everyday life. Elon thought he better not waste years doing PhD and miss out on all the opportunities the Internet represented. He wanted to be a part of it. Whether he made money or not was immaterial. He just wanted to be a part of building the Internet.

His first attempt at joining the Internet party was to look for a job at Netscape, one of the first successful Internet companies. He did not get any response, perhaps because he did not have a degree in computer. He went to the company's office and hung out in the lobby, looking for someone to talk to. But he was too scared to approach anyone. He returned empty-handed.

Unable to find a job, his only choice was to make a job for himself by building a company. He convinced his brother Kimbal to join him in the venture. Along with another friend, the three partners created a company called Zip2 which was initially called Global Link Information Network. It was essentially a searchable business directory with maps.

The start, however, was rough. None of the three partners had much money. Elon was actually on the negative, with a pile of student loan in his name. They did not have enough money to rent an apartment and an office. It was actually cheaper to rent an office than an apartment. Elon and his brother slept on the office couch that functioned as a bed at night. For shower, they would go to the local YMCA.

Their financial situation was so bad that they could afford only computer. Theirs was essentially a one-computer company. The computer hosted their website by day. By night, their website was turned off for Elon to code. Zip2 and its founders worked like this for seven days a week.

As Elon dreamed, Zip2 did contribute to the Internet's growth in its early days. Web advertisement was never heard of before but

Zip2 showed the way. It also helped many newspapers shift to the electronic format. These were highly innovative in those days.

The biggest challenge, of course, was getting customers. That was particularly difficulty because not many people and fewer businesses understood what the Internet even meant.

In the following years, hedge fund and private equity funds came forward with funding for Zip2. It expanded and became a success. In 1999, Compaq Computer bought Zip2 for $307 million from which Elon's share was around $22 million. It was a lot of money and Elon was left scratching his head over why someone would pay that kind of money for such a small company.

If it was someone else, such a windfall would have been enough to stop working and lead a comfortable life without having to worry about another thing. But not Elon. He moved to his next project. A big project.

When we learn about this leg of Elon's life journey, there is one point that may be of help to the rest of us. Elon did not drop out of his PhD program and start a company with a rock-solid confidence about its success. In fact, when he started it out, of the many outcomes he saw, success was only one of the possible outcomes. In other word, complete failure of the project was something Elon was ready to accept. This mindset is extremely important for any entrepreneur.

What prevents most of us from starting something new, from taking risk and going into the unknown, is our fear of failure. When this fear exists sufficiently, it always wins and we stop from going forward. In the end, our fear keeps us from trying out anything new. We are failure-averse beings, meaning we do not like failures. But people like Elon Musk are different. When they look at a project, they see a range of possible outcomes. Failure and success are two of the many possible outcomes. It now appears quite evident that inventors like Elon just go out and try, accepting fully that failure is one possibility. Rather than the possibility of failure holding them back, they go ahead and try things out. This is an important mindset we could benefit from adopting.

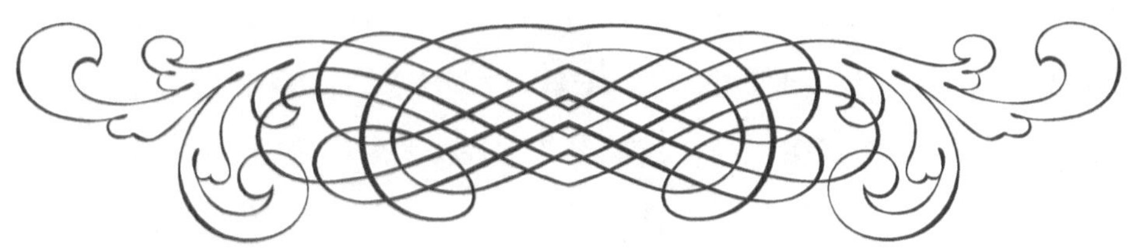

V. PAYPAL

When Elon was in college, he read about the world's fastest street-legal car then – the McLaren F1. He was fascinated by it – the car was just perfect in every sense. He promised himself that if he ever made enough money, he would buy a McLaren F1. At the time, there were only 62 F1s in the world. The price for one car? A cool $1 million.

From the sale of his first company Zip2 to Compaq, Elon Musk earned $22 million. He spent $1 million from it on a McLaren F1.

Just four years before that, Elon was sleeping on an office couch and taking shower in YMCA. From the comfort of a couch bed to the plush interiors of F1 in four years, Elon had definitely made it in the land of dreams.

Even with his million-dollar purchase, Elon still had a lot of cash left. $20 million is a huge pile of cash for any individual to have. Elon had the choice of taking the cash and going to Bahamas where he could buy an island and spend the rest of his life by a nice beach, sipping cocktails, without having to worry about money ever again. But the idea of lying on a beach the whole day was the worst for someone like Elon. It was a horrible idea.

After the sale of his first company, Elon did not take any time off to celebrate his newfound status as the newest millionaire in Silicon Valley. In fact, even before he sold his first company, he was thinking of his next project. A little more than a month later, Elon was de in his new project. This time it was finance.

When Elon thought about it, he saw that financial services had a lot of room for innovation by using the power of the Internet. Firstly, money is just numbers. When money changes hands, it is actually the numbers going from one account to the other. Paper money is a small fraction of all the money there is out there; the vast majority of money exists simply as numbers.

Secondly, transferring digits from one account to the other – which is what money transfer is actually all about – takes very low bandwidth. The Internet speed was an issue those days – downloading a 10-minute HD YouTube video would have taken a full day, sometimes even more, with the best connection, provided there were no disconnections in between. Disconnections of course happened a lot and when that happened, you had to go back to the beginning to restart the process, sometimes after 99.6 percent of the download was complete. And the Internet of the day did not really have HD videos. Since transferring digits does not consume a lot of bandwidth, Elon thought it would be viable.

Thirdly, in the pre-internet era, financial transactions were very slow. If someone ordered a thing over phone, they would have to mail the checks through the post office. To complete a single transaction, it took weeks and months. The Internet would help speed up financial transaction. People with credit cards were a little better off but there was a downside to credit card transactions those days. Whenever they made a purchase, people had to share their credit card details over the phone. There was a slight problem of losing a lot of money if the details went to the wrong people. Scammers included.

Lastly, customers often had to maintain multiple accounts with multiples banks and financial service providers. For example, you had bank account with one bank but your investment account would be with another bank or brokerage firm, and your insurance with yet another firm.

Elon thought that he could combine all the financial and banking services required by a person in one place. The person can manage all his accounts from one place and make it easy for the person to manage his mortgage, credit card, insurance and so on. He called his company X.com.

A common question people ask is, how did he make the jump from starting a city guide to a finance company?

For one, Elon has a degree in finance from the famous Wharton college of UPenn. Secondly, Elon by then had some taste of banking, having worked as an intern at a bank in Canada. How he got this internship is quite interesting.

Soon after Elon reached Canada, his brother Kimbal followed him there. The two, always good friends, did a lot of things together. One thing they particularly enjoyed doing was finding interesting people to meet. They scoured newspapers looking for these people. Then they took turns calling these people to ask if they would meet the two brothers for lunch. Those phone calls were part prank and part harassment.

One of the people they harassed was a marketing manager for a sports team, a writer and an executive of the Bank of Nova Scotia, Peter Nicholson. It took them six months to get a lunch appointment, but the two brothers did get an appointment with Peter. When the lunch was over, Elon had impressed Peter that he earned himself a summer internship at the bank as an adviser to Peter.

It was during this internship that Elon got a taste of banking. But most importantly, he came to the simple realization that bankers were essentially filthy rich and filthy dumb. It took only an intern earning fourteen dollars an hour to find a massive opportunity for the banks to make billions overnight but the bankers simply refused to grab the opportunity. Elon would later look back at such moments when he was working on X.com and get renewed confidence to succeed.

But if a summer internship and a finance degree are all that were required to start a bank, there would be a swarm of people doing it. Going into his new banking project, however, those where what Elon more or less had: a short internship and a degree. Where and how would he make the start into this labyrinth called internet banking? In a typical Elon Musk way, he ordered a book on banking to learn about the inner workings of the bank.

This did little to boost the confidence of his small team of engineers trying to launch an online bank. Every day, as they learnt more about banking, they sunk deeper into the mystery. For one, they had to deal with a hundred and one regulations that are there just to prevent someone from starting a bank. But with Elon's perseverance, the company got a banking license, formed partnership with a big bank, and developed a complete online financial system. X.com went online in November in 1999, a day before Thanksgiving. In the lead up to the launch, Elon stayed in the office for forty-eight hours straight.

One of the services Elon started in X.com was to use email addresses to make payments. This was radical at a time when the only way customers could make payments was to cut a check or give their credit card details over phone or the Internet. This service revolutionized online payment and X.com attracted more than 200,000 customers in a few months.

Around the same time, another company called Confinity was building a service to enable users to make payments between PDAs, the hand-held mini computers. They called their service PayPal.

For a while, X.com and Confinity raced and competed fiercely to be the market leader in online payments. But seeing no point in trying to beat each other, the two companied decided to merge in March 2000. The merged company kept the name X.com but their main service of online payment was called PayPal. As the largest shareholder, Elon became the CEO of the new company.

Soon after the merger, however, problems erupted. The teams from X.com and Confinity could not get along; they wanted to use different technology platforms. The company could not keep up with exploding customer base and their website kept crashing. With online payment, fraud mushroomed, draining huge amount of money, and the company could not seem to stop it. With the company facing multiple problems, people began losing faith in their leader: Elon.

Then it happened. In September 2000, Musk went on a honeymoon with his wife Justine to Australia, nine months after their marriage. Some unhappy board members jumped into the opportunity of Elon's absence and launched a coup, replacing Elon as the CEO with one of the founders of Confinity.

After he was sacked as the CEO of the company, Elon stayed on as an adviser. In July 2002, eBay offered to buy the company which was then known as PayPal for $1.5 billion. As the biggest shareholder, Elon earned $250 million from the sale.

McLaren F1

McLaren F1 is a sports car designed and manufactured by British car manufacturer McLaren Cars. In 1998, McLaren set the Guinness World Record for the world's fastest production car after it reached a speed of 240.1 miles per hour. It takes only 3.2 seconds for the car to do zero to 60. One of the other unique features about F1 is that it has three seats: driver's seat in the middle and two passenger seats on either side slightly to the back. It is considered one of the finest cars, and by car enthusiasts as the purest super car, to be ever produced. Only 106 of them were produced.

Elon nearly did not get his F1. Fashion designer Ralph Lauren was also interested in buying it but Elon beat him by an hour. Elon got the 67th car. One of the other fortunate owners of this piece of engineering marvel is Rowan Atkinson aka Mr. Bean.

But Elon nearly lost his life in this beast. In 2000, Elon was driving his F1 to meet a venture capitalist. Along with him in the car was his business partner at PayPal, Peter Thiel. To show the car's power, Elon floored the gas pedal and the car roared. But during a lane change, Elon lost control and the car began to spin. The McLaren F1 slammed into an embankment of the road which sent the car flying into air.

When it crashed to the grown, Elon was laughing hysterically. When asked by Peter what he was laughing at, Elon replied: "You don't know the funny part, it wasn't even insured".

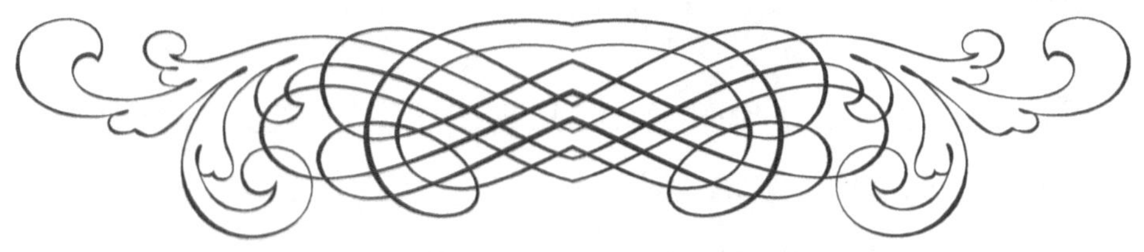

VI. AIMING FOR MARS

When Elon Musk was sacked as the CEO of X.com, it felt like a punch in the gut. He tried to fight the board's coup and get back his position, but by the time he returned from Sydney, Australia, things had moved on and he was no longer the boss of X.com. Elon was angry and resentful but he decided to stomach the punch and move on without putting up a serious fight in the interest of the company.

With the responsibilities of managing the company taken away, he was left with time to explore other ideas. This time, he turned to his childhood fascination: space. As a child, Elon was thrilled by science fictions about interstellar travels where humans were not just a single-planet species but star farers and a multiplanetary species.

At first, he did not think he could do much for space exploration. After all, space is so vast and it requires technology and resources which only rich governments have. He thought that even a person as motivated as himself could do little to conquer space. He imagined that NASA would have some plans on space exploration. Perhaps, he can have a look at how he can contribute to NASA's own plans.

Upon looking through NASA's website, however, Elon was disappointed to discover that NASA had no plans whatsoever of sending people to the Moon, let alone to Mars. In 1970s, there was a lot of excitement around sending people to Mars. The first landing of two men on the Moon on July 20, 1969 had filled people with hope and imagination of going farther away from Earth into space. Unfortunately, by the time Elon visited NASA website in 2001, those dreams of 1970s no longer existed.

This struck Elon hard. After the technological feat of the Moon landing, landing people on Mars seemed like a real possibility. In 1970s, if you asked people what was possible by 2010, they would have said that a human mission to Mars was more viable than an iPhone. However, while smart phones had become a reality, space technologies had not progressed. In fact, Elon was disappointed that space exploration technology had reached its pinnacle during the Apollo mission to the Moon and since then had gone backward instead of progressing forward.

He believed that the very idea of the nation of the United States is intertwined with exploration, starting with the establishment of colonies in the new world, and then conquering the vast and deadly frontiers by early settlers. With most part of the surface of the Earth explored, space is the next frontier but America did not seem to have a plan to conquer it.

Elon was quite bothered by the lack of push for space exploration. He assumed that humanity as a whole had lost interest in exploring the farther reaches of our solar system and in fact the Galaxy, and that a dream had died. The science fiction he read as a child had remained a fiction. He wanted to change it.

His initial plan was never to launch a space company. He thought space exploration was beyond the means of any one individual or even a company. All he wanted to do was to get people excited about space exploration once again. He assumed that if people are excited enough about it, there would be more support for NASA to get more funding from the government. Therefore, his plan was to simply reignite a dream.

To get this plan going, his first idea was called Mars Oasis. He thought that people would get excited about Mars once again if he could somehow manage to land a small robotic land rover and a small greenhouse with dormant seeds on the surface of Mars. The seeds would then be hydrated with nutrient rich water and they start growing. It would make a perfect photo: a green plant growing on the red planet. And it would in fact be the first life on another planet that we know of.

By that time, Elon had a bit of cash. He had earned $180 million from the sale of PayPal to eBay. He thought that he would spend half of that money on his Mars Oasis mission. He would still have the other half to live on.

Business wise, his Mars Oasis mission would be a 100 percent loss. He did not expect any return. He just thought that his Mars mission was important and if it resulted in one day people going to Mars, it would be a good return on his investment.

He read whatever he could about space and talked to experts. He got hold of the best aerospace, electrical and civil engineers, and physicists. Through this process, Musk devoured all information he required to start his Mars Oasis mission. He came to the conclusion that sending a mission to Mars can be made cost effective, and that he can do it well within his allocated budget of around $90 million. But there was a hurdle on the way and he could not quite overcome it: Rockets.

To escape the Earth's gravitational pull and enter space, the only technology available is rocket. Elon would need rockets to take his mission to Mars but the rockets that were available in the market was very expensive. The cost of one rocket alone came to $65 million. That was a non-starter.

Unable to find any affordable rockets in the US, Elon and his team went to Russia. They were looking for Inter-Continental Ballistic Missiles or ICBM for short. ICBM are not meant to go to space. Instead, their primary purpose is to carry nuclear weapons. They are very powerful and very fast.

The cost of ICBM was much cheaper at around $10 million per piece. Elon reached an agreement with Russian military to buy a few ICBM. But he saw a problem. The supply of ICBM was small, and if Elon needed more of it in the future, he would have to pay far more than $10 million. He decided against buying rockets from Russia. Another solution would have to be found.

In searching for this solution, Elon had to turn to his model of thinking he uses to learn and solve problems. It comes from physics and is called reasoning from first principles. The method is simple: break everything down to their smallest components and then build from there. If you are learning something, you first need to fully grasp the most basic principles and laws, before you learn higher level stuffs. If you are building a house, for example, you start by first understanding the materials that go into building a house. When Elon thought about the price of the rockets, he broke down and studied the cost of all the components that go into building a rocket. What he found surprised him.

He discovered that it would be far cheaper to build the rockets himself. The cost of material and labor to build a rocket would only be around $6.5 million which is one-tenth of the cost of Boeing's rockets. Why were their rockets so expensive? Because they did not build the rockets themselves; they got their rocket components from different suppliers, each supplier charging commission and jacking up prices.

Upon arriving in the US, Elon met his team. They decided to build rockets themselves.

Why Space? The Thinking Behind the Journey Into Space

With so much problem there to be solved on the face of Earth, putting so much effort and resources into going to space seems like priority gone awry. It appears like an expensive pet project done to get some thrill out of it, something that has no real use for other people. But apart from chasing his childhood fantasy, Elon Musk has some serious reasons for aiming for Mars.

Our solar system formed around 4.5 billion years ago. Planet Earth also came into existence around that same time. About 3.7 billion years ago, life took hold in the form of single-cellular bacteria. This simple life form evolved into complex organisms some 1.6 billion years ago. Humans came into the scene much, much later, about 315,000 years ago.

But life on Earth is not guaranteed. In fact, during the course of the evolution of life, there were about twelve mass extinction events that wiped out life from the face of the planet. The mass extinction event that occurred 65 million years ago killed all dinosaurs and millions of other plant and animal species. These mass extinction events are preserved in the fossils for us to see.

The next mass extinction event will happen. And this time, the human species will be on the line. When it comes to mass extinction events, it is never a question of if it will occur. The only question is when and from where. It is possible humans could cause it. But there are so many ways for life on Earth to go back to zero. Something bad is bound to happen. A wayward asteroid that is big enough can split Earth into fragments. One day, the Sun, will run out of hydrogen to fuse and the Sun will collapse into a supernova, the force from which will blow up all the planets into atoms. This are life cycles of stars and planets, a universal law in its truest sense. How can humans rise above this predicament?

Humans are the only confirmed intelligent beings in the known universe. If there are other intelligent beings inhabiting distant planets – which is a possibility if we look at the number of stars and galaxies in the universe – we do not know yet. And looking from Earth, only humans have the ability to make life multiplanetary. A chimpanzee, for instance, has not yet learnt to make fire let alone build a rocket. The responsibility of taking life across planets and stars fall squarely on humans.

But humans evolved into the current form only around 315,000 years ago. In the timescale of our solar system, that period is just a tiny, tiny bleep. We learnt to store knowledge in written words about 10,000 years ago. And it was not until the last century that humans developed the technology to fly to our nearest extra-terrestrial destination, the Moon. Even if we are able to guarantee life on this planet for the next 315,000 years, in the larger scheme of things, 600,000 years is still just a tiny bleep. The question is how can humans use our intelligence and consciousness to propagate life so that life as a whole has multiple bases spread across the universe.

The next question is: why do it now? Elon's answer is that we do it now because the window to the outer space is now open, for the very first time. This window of opportunity is made possible by all the technologies that exist and will come into existence as we work earnestly toward it. Technology on its own will not grow; in fact, it will degrade. Look at all the technologies used by ancient civilizations that we forgot: the pyramid, the aqueducts and so on. It can only grow through investment of human intelligence and effort. Elon believes the opportunity to aim for Mars and beyond is now because like ancient civilizations we may lose even the existing technologies if we don't act now.

In going for space exploration, it is not just about sending people out of Earth in spaceships. Elon's main motivation is to get people excited about life and living.

To think on the scale of humanity and evolution of life takes boldness, something that Elon is not short on. However, not everyone shares such a bold vision. There are always people who have difficulty seeing beyond the present challenges and these people sometime can kill dreams. They mean well but they do not see as far as the visionary sees.

When Elon and his team were discussing about building rockets, some well-meaning friends thought Elon was crazy. They thought he would be wasting his money on rockets and they tried their best to stop him. One time, a group of them compiled video clips of rockets exploding and going up in flames and forced Elon to watch it.

What his friends did not know was he was not going into rocket business for money. They saw Elon's interest in space only through the amount dollars he would burn. But Elon had already calculated and come to the conclusion that his Mars mission would be a hundred percent loss. He wasn't expecting to make money out of this mission. When you expect nothing, you lose nothing. Whatever you gain out of it is pure gain. That is why, Elon was unfazed by friends trying to change his mind.

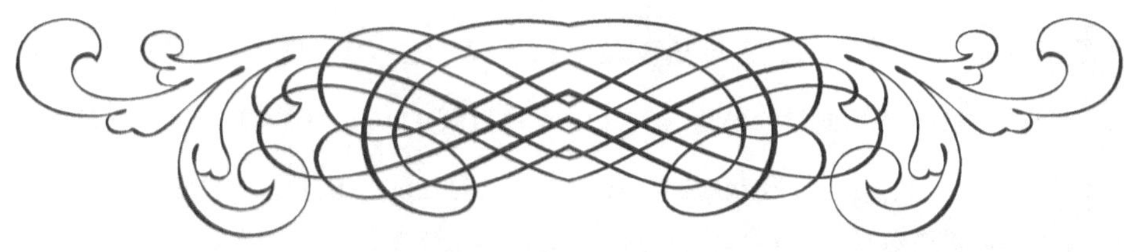

VII. THE ROAD TO LIFTOFF

After Elon and his team failed to find cheap rockets for their Mars mission, they decided to build their own rockets from scratch. They named the company Space Exploration Technologies or SpaceX. Elon's fascination with the letter X is something we can't grasp but that is not important.

To fund the company, Elon threw $100 million from the money he got from the sale of PayPal to eBay. He learnt bitter lessons from his previous two companies and he did not ever want to give control of his company to other investors. He wanted to keep the company's control which gave him the power to do what he saw fit for the company.

When Elon started SpaceX in June 2002, it was not as if he knew what he was doing. Far from it. All he knew was he wanted to contribute to space exploration and that this required rockets. What kind of rockets? He had no clue.

Elon first had to put together a team. Rocket

 science is not easy and it would take a team of highly knowledgeable people to build anything remotely resembling a rocket to shoot people out into the space. Elon went on a headhunt to get the best people in the industry to come and work for him. He convinced top engineers from big aerospace industries like Boeing to leave their boring jobs and join him in his exciting venture. He would go to universities and recruit top students. It is said that Elon personally interviewed every employee of SpaceX, which now totals 12,000 people.

Elon was doing his own part. He has a physics degree but that is not rocket science. At the same time, he just did not want to be a CEO of SpaceX. He had to contribute significantly to the development of the company and its technologies. Therefore, Elon had to learn everything about rockets. He turned to reading and devoured information from every book and Russian rocket manuals he could put his hand on. In the end, he was not just the CEO of SpaceX. He was also its chief engineer.

The company set up its new factory in Los Angeles in an old warehouse. It was designed to have an open workflow where designers, engineers, managers, welders and everyone worked together. Structure defines efficiency and a classic mistake in most companies is putting people into groups. This creates silos, communication issues, divisions and cubicle mindset among groups simply by putting them in different cubicles.

The vision for the company was to build cheap and efficient rockets. Until SpaceX joined the rocket business, aerospace companies built only very expensive rockets for maximum performance. Every rocket was a Ferrari. SpaceX's goal was to build the rocket equivalent of Honda Accord, reliable but cheaper rockets. Before SpaceX, a rocket carrying a payload of 550 pound to the space would cost $30 million. Elon promised his rockets would carry 1,400 pounds for $6.9 million. Elon declared that SpaceX's first rocket would be called Falcon 1, a tribute to Star Wars.

Elon is known for many things but patience? No. He needed to move fast and he expected everyone in his team to keep up with him. He set extremely ambitious target for his first rocket. His goals were to finish building the rocket engine in May 2003, a second engine in June, the body by August, assembly by September and the first launch in November 2003. In other words, from the company's founding to the first rocket launch, his team had around 15 months.

Very soon, Elon's space mission caught the attention of space enthusiasts, businesses, scientists and even the US military. Everyone had been dreaming of a day when custom built satellites could be designed, built and sent to the space in matter of months and not the ten years it took then. That was being done by a private individual, and not the government or big multinational companies, made it even more exciting.

Falcon 1 was a two-stage rocket launch vehicle. It is essentially one rocket stacked on another. During the liftoff from the launchpad, the first stage rocket would ignite and would have to burn for 180 seconds and reach speed of 6,850 miles per hour for the launch vehicle to reach space. After entering space, the first stage rocket would separate and the second stage would ignite. The second stage would reach speed of 17,000 miles per hour for the launch vehicle to enter orbit.

SpaceX designed Falcon 1 to deliver a payload of 1000 KG into low Earth orbit, the space between an altitude of 99 miles and 1200 miles above the Earth's surface. With a lighter payload, Falcon 1 should even able to reach the cislunar space, a space between the Earth and the Moon. By comparison, the International

Space Station circulates the Earth at 250 miles above the Earth's surface.

Each of the two rockets in Falcon 1 had separate engines. In a rocket, designing and building the engines are the most complex part of the project just like in a car. If the engine is faulty, the rocket is going nowhere.

The team at SpaceX called the engine of Falcon 1's first stage rocket Merlin and the engine of the second stage Kestrel, both names referring to two types of falcon. Initially, SpaceX tried to get the various components for their rockets from different suppliers. But buying from others was expensive and time consuming. Their only choice was to build almost everything themselves from scratch.

Under the watchful eyes and sometimes angry words of their CEO, workers at SpaceX pushed their limits every working day to build the rockets. Despite pushing their boundaries to the maximum, they missed Elon's initial deadline of November 2003 for the first launch.

Finally, on March 24, 2006, Falcon 1 was ready for the launch. It was the fastest launch vehicle development in the history, going from design to the launchpad in three years. The launch site was a military base in a remote island called Kwaj in the Pacific Ocean belonging to Marshall Islands. Elon and his brother Kimbal joined the SpaceX team to watch the launch. Joining them were also representatives from government and corporations.

At first everything went as expected. There was the ignition and liftoff. For twenty-five long seconds, Falcon 1 pierced through the atmosphere as expected. Then a fire broke out above the Merlin engine. The machine started spinning furiously and began tumbling back to Earth. Falcon 1 crashed back on the launchpad. The payload actually landed right in machine shop of SpaceX. All the blood, sweat and tear that went into building the rocket were gone in exactly 33 seconds.

The team at SpaceX was devastated by the failure. Blames were exchanged and some people were left red-faced and fuming. Investigations later found out that the failure was caused by a corroded fuel pipe nut.

The cost of the failure was huge. Elon was stuffed with cash but every rocket burnt through millions of dollars. How many more rocket launches can SpaceX have before they ran out of cash? Elon was ready for failure but how many failed launches can he endure before he was forced to close shop?

However, Elon remained undisturbed by the failed launch. He was prepared to fail. Soon after the first Falcon 1 blew up, the team at SpaceX was back, building their second rocket.

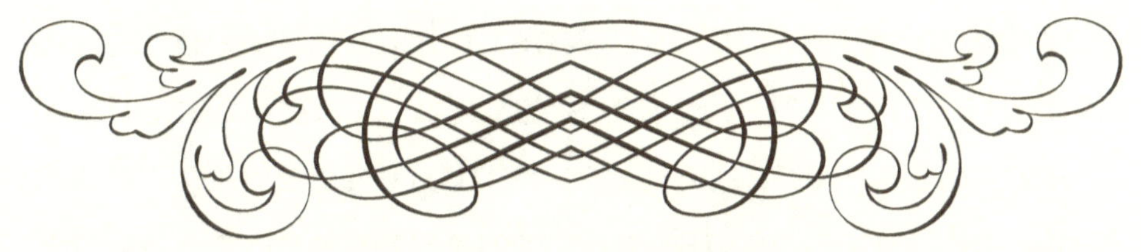

VIII. TESLA – ELECTRIFYING PERSONAL CARS

When Elon was studying at Queen's in Canada, he hosted a birthday party at his apartment. One of the invitees was a girl called Christie, daughter of Peter Nicholson, the executive at the Bank of Nova Scotia who offered Elon a summer internship. Elon had never met Christie before. When they met, Elon's first lines for Christie was: "I think a lot about electric cars. Do you think about electric cars?"

This line of questioning failed to electrify the young girl, and Elon is said to have since then modified his pick-up line.

But one thing is for certain: Electric cars filled a sizeable part of Elon's thoughts and imagination from his younger days.

For Elon, electric car was a logical step in the evolution of personal transportation. Combustion engine cars require gas and diesel. But petroleum is a finite resource, which means if we keep on consuming it, it will one day run out. Petroleum is not a renewable resource. As countries develop and people become richer, more people can afford and will buy cars. This would put more demand for gas and diesel. With faster consumption, the world will run out of gas and diesel faster. Then what happens when the world runs out of gas and diesel to power cars and the economy?

The only way to prevent this from happening is to use renewable fuel for cars. Electricity is a renewable resource because it can be generated from water, wind and the Sun. All these sources of electricity will not run out, unlike fossil fuels like gas.

Big car companies like General Motors did make electric cars when they were forced by the law to make cars fueled by renewable energy. GM's first electric car called EV1 worked well and people loved it. But when the law was quashed after lawsuits from car companies, GM recalled all its electric cars despite protest from consumers and crushed them in a junkyard.

For any electric car, the biggest problem was the battery. A gasoline car can run up to 400 miles on a single tank of gas. If a car has to be refueled every 50 miles, it becomes a burden for the driver. For an electric car, this kind of range was not possible because the battery could not hold enough power to take the car this far.

Then in early 2003, someone replaced the lead acid battery with lithium ion battery and made an electric car. The car went from 0 to 60 miles in under four seconds, which only high-performance, sports cars could do. With one charge, the car could travel for up to 250 miles.

The prototype was primitive but it proved that lithium ion batteries, the kind used in laptops and phones, can make electric cars possible.

In 2003, Elon was neck-deep in his new project: SpaceX. In the fall that year, Elon was introduced to an entrepreneur called Straubel who wanted to make electric planes and electric cars. Elon did not like the idea of electric planes but electric car was an instant hit with him. He agreed to give $10,000 from a $100,000 required by Straubel for his electric car project.

At around the same time, two men by the names Eberhard and Tarpenning were working on their own electric car using lithium ion batteries in Northern California. They incorporated their company in July 2003. They called it Tesla, a respect to the one of the most famous inventors in the human history, Nikola Tesla.

Upon learning about the new company, Elon told Straubel to meet the founders of Tesla. The three men instantly decided to work together to build an electric car.

Like all groundbreaking innovations, when Tesla first announced plans to make electric cars, people laughed at the idea. Starting a car company was itself an outrageous idea. And people had reasons to doubt. Before Tesla joined the auto industry, the newest car company in the US was Chrysler. It was started in 1925. This shows the challenges of starting a car company, a successful car company. But starting a successful electric car company? That was just crazy.

It was an uphill task for Tesla. To start off with, lithium ion batteries can explode. The Tesla Roadster, the first production car of the company, had close to 7000 individual batteries. An explosion of a battery pack this size would definitely rip the car apart and kill the people inside it. If a Tesla were to explode, it would kill the company altogether before it even began. Through trial and error, and many explosions later, the engineers at Tesla were able to reduce the risk of batteries exploding to an acceptable level.

The second challenge was the price. The price

for Tesla's earliest model was more than $100,000. As the company started with their first car, the cost estimate per car crossed $200,000 mark. There are not many buyers who can throw so much money for a car. At that price, Tesla would never really become an alternative for most consumers.

In addition, the company had to deal with a hundred other problems. A lot of technologies required to make the car was non-existent. The team at Tesla had to create them. The company missed many deadlines to bring out their first production cars. Partners failed to deliver. Regulatory requirements further added to the cost. The company was bleeding money and unable to find new sources to top up.

Elon's early role in Tesla was as one of the funders. No one thought electric cars were possible. Therefore, no one wanted to put money into it. Elon was the earliest investor, in total investing around $70 million from his PayPal money in the early days of Tesla. This made Elon the largest shareholder and the chairman of Tesla.

Once he became a part of the company, Elon was fully into the company. He took the responsibility of hiring and firing people. Most importantly, he was one of the main brains behind Tesla's sleek design. Prototype electric cars before Tesla were ugly and looked like cardboard cars. Elon wanted Tesla cars to be functional, sporty and cool all around. He wanted a Tesla to be not just a car but the car.

To make Tesla cars more affordable, Elon published his "secret" plan for Tesla in 2006: build expensive sports cars. Use that money to build affordable cars. Use that money to build even more affordable cars. It was a business strategy that worked for Tesla.

It started with Roadster – sleek and sporty in every sense but fully electric. With innovative promotions, the first prototypes of the car caught public imagination and soon became the talk of the town. Even though there were delays in delivering the car, Tesla lived up to the hype by producing the first road-worthy, fully electric Roadster in 2008, the first car going to Elon.

Along the way, Elon took tough decisions to prevent the company from going under. Eberhard, one of the co-founders and the brain behind Tesla, was the founding CEO. His contribution to the company goes beyond ideas and technology. But as the company got bigger, he was no longer suitable to lead it. He made some terrible decisions that affected the company. As the chairman, Elon sacked Eberhard from the position of CEO. Elon took over as the CEO in late 2008. Tesla owes its strong global brand to its co-founder Musk.

Tesla Dealership

Tesla's innovation did not stop with their cars. It extended to how cars are sold to the buyers. Before Tesla came, buying a car was a pain. You would go to a local car dealer and bargain your way to the right price. The experience of car buying would leave most buyers feeling a little bit cheated. Tesla wanted to change it.

Instead of using third-party dealers, Tesla sells cars directly through its website and own showrooms, often located within shopping malls. Buying a Tesla is as easy as buying, say an iPhone. In fact, Tesla showrooms are the Apple Stores of cars. Cutting out the middleman means better buying experience for the customer.

Many states in the US, however, have laws that prohibits car manufacturers from selling directly to customers. They can sell only through dealerships. In these states, customers end up paying more for the same car.

Tesla's marketing ingenuity is equally compelling. You will never see a Tesla advertisement. Elon does not believe in marketing. He thinks that if you build a good enough product, it will market itself. You only need to watch all those rave reviews of Tesla owners to see how true this is.

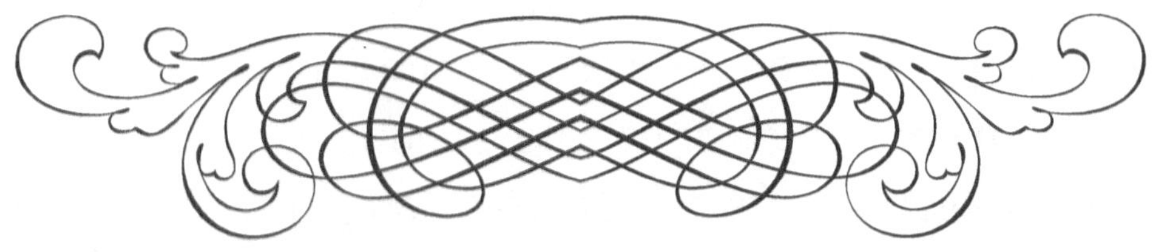

IX. CRISIS

In an epic tale, the hero goes through a challenge so big that it can kill her. This challenge is so great that it appears like the entire world conspires to kill the hero. To come out of it, the hero must gather every last nerve she has and face the challenge head on. Otherwise, the hero dies and the story ends in a tragedy.

Elon faced this moment in 2008. It was his walk through the valley of death. Everything around him appeared to be collapsing. He edged towards a total wipeout.

After the first failure of Falcon 1 launch in 2006, the team at SpaceX made frantic effort to have the second launch before the end of the year. After a series of delays, the second launch finally took place in March 2007. There was a successful liftoff and the first stage of the rocket performed well. But a malfunction in the separation stage sent the second stage of the rocket out of control. It was lost and even the wreckage could not be recovered. Along with the rocket, its payload of satellites was also lost in space. The failure was another big blow to SpaceX.

But if you haven't failed for a third time, it is not really a failure. And that is what happened with Falcon 1. The third launch in August 2008 also failed. The first stage rocket failed to stop in time and instead continued pushing the second stage rocket. Along with NASA's satellites, the third Falcon 1 rocket was carrying ashes of 208 people whose last wish was to be launched into space. One of those people was Star Trek actor James Doohan.

With each failure, public skepticism grew and people at SpaceX were looking at the death of company. For the first time, they began to despair. And there were reasons for it. Workers at SpaceX had been putting up 80 hours a week to make the launch a success. The company was going bankrupt.

Elon tried to dissipate the despair of his employees. After the third failure, he wrote an e-mail to them:

We knew this was going to be hard, it is after all rocket science. The most important message I'd like to send right now is that SpaceX will not skip a beat in execution going forward. There should be absolutely zero question that SpaceX will prevail in reaching orbit and demonstrating reliable space transport. For my part, I will never give up and I mean never. Thanks for your hard work and now on to flight four.

This message changed the mood of the workers. But behind his brave face and optimism, Elon was fully aware of the trouble SpaceX was in. The rockets had burnt through all the cash from PayPal he put aside for it and some more. If the next launch failed, it would be the end of SpaceX.

On September 28, 2008, SpaceX made its fourth, and potentially the last attempt, at sending Falcon 1 to the orbit. The hopes, dreams and pride of everyone who worked on the project was riding on this launch. It was either a make or a break deal. Fortunately, the launch was a success.

It took six year – four more than Elon's first estimate – for SpaceX to reach this goal. When it did, it was nothing short of a modern miracle. The first time ever for a private company to achieve such a feat of sending rocket to orbit, a feat otherwise reserved only for a few wealthy countries.

For Elon, however, the victory was short-lived. SpaceX, even while they were working on Falcon 1, was already working on another more powerful launch vehicle. They had also started working on Dragon capsules that would one day take cargo and astronauts to the International Space Station. These automatically led to more expenditure as workers and materials required grew. SpaceX was running out of cash. Fast.

On the other side, Tesla was not doing any better either. It had failed to deliver its first car, Roadster, due to technical challenges and some poor decisions along the way. The team had to go back to the drawing board when they were supposed to deliver the cars to the customers. In the meanwhile, Tesla too was guzzling whatever money it had in its account. As the CEO of two companies, both of which appeared to be going nowhere, Elon was under the kind of stress not many mortals can handle. At the same time, his personal life was going through a turmoil.

Elon married his college sweetheart Justine in 2000. The couple went through a lot since their marriage. Elon got thrown out of PayPal when they were on honeymoon. Their firstborn son died very soon after birth in 2002, which was obviously very painful for both Elon and Justine. Elon refused to talk about it until much later, and when he did the pain he felt at losing a child was like any other parent. In the years that followed, they had a twin and a triplet. The Musks exploded but Elon was mostly absent from parenting, as he shuttled between the two headquarters of SpaceX and Tesla, separated by 400 miles. All of these did not make it easy for Elon and Justine. They got divorced in June 2008.

The divorce, however, turned ugly. Justine fought for every last dollar she could get out of the divorce settlement. She also wanted a Tesla Roadster as a part of it. Elon refused the demands, for one he no longer had cash with him. All of them were taken up by his two companies. Once the settlement was done, Justine turned to media to talk about Elon, and she did not have many good things to say about him. Elon's image of a serial entrepreneur working for the betterment of the humanity was challenged and he became the target for all sorts of attacks, some deeply personal.

2008 was the year that both Tesla and SpaceX were on the verge of bankruptcy, and Musk needed no more negative publicity for any of his two companies. But when misfortune comes, it rains. In all this chaos, it appeared that some people were simply out there to get Elon. And these people came from every corner like vultures preying on a victim who had fallen on tough times.

For Tesla, one such person was the presenter of a hit television show called Top Gear. Jeremy Clarkson's review was that the Tesla Roadster can do only 50 miles on one charge, that it would take 25 days to recharge the car using a small wind turbine and that you would need two Roadsters, one for driving and the other to sit in the garage charging. At a time when there were a lot of Tesla doubters, Clarkson's review rubbed salt on the wound.

Clarkson's negative review was deliberate and was meant to be a lie. A Tesla engineer found a script used by Clarkson. Even before getting into the Roadster, Clarkson was supposed to say: ""In the real world, it doesn't seem to work".

Then there was a columnist of The New York Times called Randall Stross. He was there launching an all-out misinformation war against Tesla and Elon. Elon appropriately called him "a huge douche bag and an idiot".

And then there were the bloggers trying to use Elon's misfortune to mint publicity for themselves. In particular, a blogger called Owen Thomas was after Elon, in part fed by his ex-wife Justine. Elon called him "The single most tediously mean-spirited person I have ever encountered." Another website began a countdown called Tesla Deathwatch.

Just as it looked like things would not get any worse, the 2008 financial crisis began. All financial market crashed. All of a sudden, things went from bleak to outright dark for Tesla, SpaceX and Elon. Cash was running out fast, and unless something happened, the life of both the companies hanged from a string.

The recession hit the car industry particularly badly. When people have no money, luxuries like cars no longer become priority. In matter of months, mammoth companies like General Motors and Chrysler went bankrupt. What chance does a startup like Tesla stand?

Elon faced the toughest choice of his life.

Divide whatever money he has between the two companies and give them a lifeline even though that may mean both companies would die when they run out of money. Or put all the money in one company, save it and let the other perish for certain. And how could he decide which company to give life and which to pull the plug? Afterall, both the companies were like his own child. Every hour, both the companies were inching towards bankruptcy and certain death. Investing his last bit of money was not a problem. The problem was which company to invest in?

It appeared everything he built and worked so hard for were just slipping away from him. In addition to the companies, there were the employees and investors he had to worry about. With all the words of his worst critics and his heroes who refused to believe in him ringing in his head, it was the first time in his life he began to doubt himself. Maybe his doubters were right after all? Even if he can bring both the companies out of danger, what next? There was nothing to show.

If SpaceX and Tesla failed, generations of

children would grow up believing they should not build electric cars or rockets. This burden weighed down heavily on Elon.

2008 was the closest Elon came to a mental breakdown. He called it the worst year of his life. Recalling the state of Elon during this time, his mother said: "I've never seen him so sad".

When Elon's Hero Failed Him

On July 20, 1969, Apollo 11 Commander Neil Armstrong became the first person to walk on the Moon. He returned from the Moon a hero, and one person who worshipped him was Elon Musk.

In a way, Elon's space ambitions came from his determination to take forward the giant step made by his hero when he walked on the Moon. However, it came as a painful shock when Armstrong testified in the US Congress that private space exploration was not yet ready.

Elon, like a kid excited to show his creation to his hero, invited Armstrong and other astronauts to visit the SpaceX factory, so show them that SpaceX can fly to space. This would remain an unfulfilled dream for Elon because Neil Armstrong died in 2012.

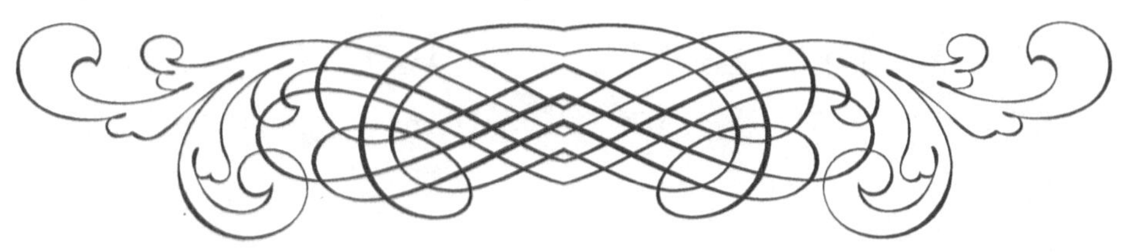

X. BACK FROM THE PRECIPICE

"When everything seems to be going against you, remember that the airplane takes off against the wind, not with it."
Henry Ford

In 2008, Elon came to the brink. To save time from commute, he slept on the factory floor and would go for days without shower. He had to borrow money from friends for rent and living expenses. Sometimes at night, he would have nightmares and scream. Of course, every now and then he would unleash his fury on his employees. As the money dried up fast, he no longer could afford to take his private jet, instead choosing a commercial airline.

In this dark, stormy phase, he picked up his favorite companion book The Hitchhiker's Guide to the Galaxy, searching for a ray of hope. And in it, he did find a quote: "Don't panic".

Elon was going through an emotional and a physiological turmoil. But he would not let his emotion make decisions for the companies. When it came to his companies' future, he returned to the calm zone, thinking things through logically, much like the Elon we see when he is asked a serious question. His ability to stay focused in the middle of a crisis is legendary.

In 2008, Tesla was burning through $4 million a month. Without a major injection of cash, the company was bound to go bust. Elon approached and begged for money from friends and anyone who could spare some cash.

Finally, in December 2008, just at the very last moment, things took a turn for the better. NASA approved a loan for SpaceX which Elon diverted to Tesla. He got $15 million from the sale of a company he had invested in called Everdream. Together, he managed to put together $20 million. He asked Tesla's existing investors to match his amount, which they did. The deal ended on Christmas Eve, hours before Tesla would have missed payment the next day and gone bankrupt.

In this crisis, Elon saw how horrible some people can be. A company called VantagePoint Capital Partners, which was an investor at Tesla, was deliberately trying to bankrupt Tesla, so that it can then make itself the largest shareholder. It could then rip open Tesla cars and sell its technologies to other car companies. This did not go down well with Elon.

Elon also saw how some people would risk it all for him. One such person was his brother Kimbal. Kimbal gave whatever he had to Tesla to the point of going himself bankrupt. Some

Tesla employees wrote checks, knowing full well they would never see their money ever again.

SpaceX also turned corner after its launch success. On December 23, 2008, NASA decided to award a contract for $1.8 billion to SpaceX to carry out twelve flights to the International Space Station.

In all, 2008 was Elon's tryst with destiny. He faced a challenge as great as his vision. He prevailed thus sealing his rightful place as an inventor, engineer, entrepreneur and a visionary the kind world is seeing for the very first time.

Today, Tesla and SpaceX have left their near-bankrupt days of 2008 far behind them. In fact, they have jumped by leaps and bounds ahead, both establishing themselves as highly valuable, pathbreaking companies. Together, they have made Elon Musk the richest man on Earth.

Tesla has come a long way from its first car, Roadster. It now has multiple sedans and crossovers: Model S, Model 3, Model X and Model Y. Tesla wanted to call Model 3 as Model E, but that name is taken by its rival Ford. Otherwise, Tesla's lineup of cars would together form SEXY. Add Roadster to it and we have SEXYR.

Tesla, however, is not stopping at passenger cars. Very soon, Tesla will have everything between electric bike, quads and electric semi. But perhaps the most exciting product to come out of Tesla will be Cybertruck. It looks like a vehicle straight out of science fiction but it is designed to be practical, efficient and plain cool like all Tesla products, capable of beating the best gasoline pickup in a tug of war. On top of that, it will be bullet proof.

What is visible in Tesla cars, however, is only one part. The invisible part of Tesla cars is even more impressive. Model S Plaid can go from 0-60 miles per hour in 1.99 seconds, making it the quickest production car, and putting to shame all other supercars. With Tesla's autopilot, you can summon your car and even take a nap while it drives you to your destination. There were rumors of the radar in

Tesla's autopilot detecting ghosts, but that is not conclusively proven. And it has the enviable title of being the safest car in the world. Tesla is definitely leading the world to a better future.

With SpaceX, Elon has crushed all doubts of skeptics and beat expectations of the best well-wishers. Falcon 1 was a test rocket, built to scale. When the fourth launch became a success, it proved that SpaceX can now scale the size of the rocket to carry real cargo. Even when Falcon 1s were crashing and burning, the engineers at SpaceX were already working on a much bigger rocket: Falcon 9. At the same time, Elon gave the go ahead to start working on the Dragon capsule which would take cargo and humans to the International Space Station.

All of these paid off. In a short few years, SpaceX achieved countless records and set a new standard in space exploration. Falcon 1 became the first privately funded fully liquid-fueled rocket to reach orbit and the first one to put a commercial satellite in orbit. In 2012, SpaceX became the first private company to send a spacecraft to the International Space Station and in 2022 the first one to send civilians. There are too many records SpaceX has achieved to list.

As in an epic tale, Elon was pushed to the breaking point and returned from it a much stronger person. Today, Elon is the face of the humanity that sees possibilities.

Starman and Roadster

In February 2018, SpaceX tried its largest and most powerful rocket yet, Falcon Heavy. With three boosters and 27 engines firing in unison, Falcon Heavy produces 5 million pounds of thrust at liftoff and is capable of launching payloads of up to 141,000 pounds into orbit. Powerful stuff.

For this maiden flight, SpaceX did not want to use real payload in case the launch did not go as expected. Instead they got a little silly and decided to send Elon's Roadster into deep space. Of course, the car needs a driver. So,

SpaceX came up with Starman – a mannequin wearing spacesuit. In case Starman and the Roadster were ever picked up by aliens, Elon had the sign "Made on Earth by humans" stamped on the Roadster. Since reaching orbit, Starman and the Roadster have been moving at the speed of 64,000 miles per hour around the Sun, making the Roadster perhaps the fastest production car ever, capable of reaching even Mars.

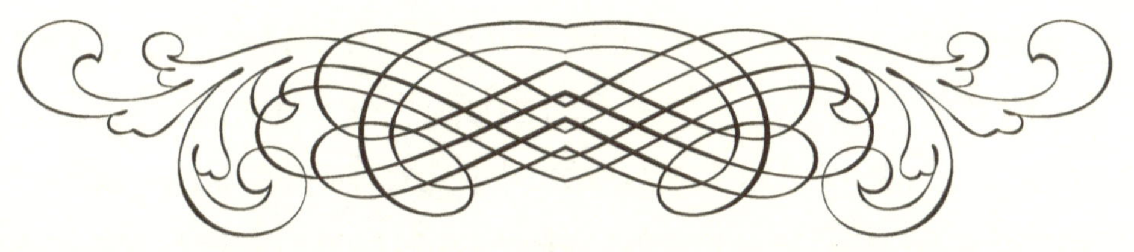

XI. THE SERIAL ENTREPRENEUR

To most people, Elon Musk is the Tesla and SpaceX guy. And rightly so because the technologies created by the two companies under his helm are truly a marvel of modern engineering and entrepreneurship. But if we know for one thing about Elon, he likes looking at big issues and taking them on. Compared to Tesla and SpaceX, his other companies look like side projects, but they are massive in their own right.

SolarCity

In 2006, Elon and two of his cousins founded a company called SolarCity while sitting together in a kitchen. Their vision was to create the most compelling energy company of the 21st century by generating cleaner and cheaper power. Where other solar companies had solar farms in deserts, SolarCity would use the roofs of homes and office building to install solar panels. They had one problem: installing solar panels is very expensive, and not many home owners can come up with the huge upfront cost.

SolarCity solved this problem by installing solar panels for free and then charging the home owners for the energy they use from the solar panels. The price home owners paid for solar power was cheaper than power from the grid which was generated using fossil fuel.

Elon provided the finance and ideas, and his cousins did the job. In a short duration, the company became one of the largest solar installers in the US.

For Tesla, SolarCity was a natural partner. A

Tesla powered fully by the Sun is Elon's idea of a renewable personal transport. Given the Sun's inexhaustible energy, compared to the mine and burn hydrocarbon feeding our economy, Elon is a big proponent of solar power. In 2016, Tesla acquired SolarCity for $2.6 billion.

Tesla is now not just a car company. It installs its proprietary solar panels and solar tiles that charge its own battery pack mounted on the wall. With this set up, homeowners have energy independence, capable of living completely off grid. In the coming years, Tesla will install solar panels generating many gigawatts of power across the US and the world, gradually but steadily replacing fossil fuel consumption at the household level. That is one step closer to Elon's goal to transition to a sustainable energy economy.

Starlink

In 2015, SpaceX started its own satellite development program. Starlink is a project to send up to 42,000 satellites to Earth's low orbit. These satellites will form a constellation that will cover the entire surface of Earth so that people can connect to the Internet from any part of the world using a Starlink dish.

In February 2022, Russia invaded Ukraine. One of its first targets was Ukraine's internet connection. Elon Musk came to the rescue with his Starlink, and Ukraine was back on line. Russia tried to disrupt Starlink internet with its electromagnetic warfare but the smart engineers at SpaceX fortified the Starlink system with a few well-placed lines of codes.

The Boring Company

By many counts, Elon Musk is the least boring person, but he plans on making boring fun. In big cities, vehicle traffic is a big issue. Countless crimes are imagined and suicidal thoughts born in the minds of people stuck in traffic in these cities. Stuck in commute is no fun, and a big waste of time. Elon plans on solving this menace by taking cars underground.

Elon announced about The Boring Company in December 2016. Cities would be connected by a network of underground tunnels fitted with electric slides that will take cars at speed of up to 120 miles per hour. Once the car reaches the destination, it would be taken up above the ground in an elevator, from where the drivers can take charge and continue to their destination.

Taking transportation underground is not a new concept. Most cities have underground passenger rail network. Taking cars underground would solve a number of issues. For one, land surface is limited. But going underground opens up so much space – there is no limit to the number of layers of tunnels that can be built underground. Secondly, the time wasted on stuck on traffic adds up to millions of manhours lost. Thirdly, cars stuck in traffic is also a huge drain on fuel and the environment.

Even in jobs as mundane as tunneling, Elon finds ways to innovate. The first step in tunneling is to excavate a large quantity of dirt to make a hole through the ground. This dirt has to be shipped to the surface, where it will take up a lot of space. Elon's idea is to convert this dirt into bricks even before it reaches the surface. As a byproduct of his tunneling, his bricks will be less than half the cost of the cheapest brick on the market but much stronger.

Taking cars underground, however, is only one part of The Boring Company. It has an even more exciting project – hyperloop. Elon first floated the idea in 2013. He said that from a physics point of view, it is possible to send a pod carrying people through a vacuum-sealed tube at speeds higher than 600 miles an hour. One of the first persons to jump at this idea was billionaire Richard Branson whose Virgin Group is already full steam into this project. But Elon is on hyperloop as well.

Neuralink

In 2016, Elon cofounded the Neuralink company with the aim of developing an interface between brain and machine. He contributed $100 million to it. The company wants to be able to implant computer chips to enhance and even restore human brain functions. For someone who suffer from brain damage, computer chips may come to the rescue if Neuralink can achieve its goals. Once the interface is developed, however, there is no limit to what can be done. Listening to music might just be a matter of connecting your head to your phone using Bluetooth.

OpenAI

Artificial Intelligence is making rapid advances. Computers are able to mimic humans thought patterns and behaviors and then react. We may make enough advances where computers are actually able to build its own intelligence. There is a cause for worry because technology can be used for good as well as for bad. Machine-gun armed drones programmed to kill is a real possibility.

To prevent such unethical development of AI while also ensuring ethical progress of AI, Elon and a few other billionaires have together committed $1 billion and created OpenAI. One of its main goals is to make AI safe.

Electric Jets

Elon is also toying with the idea of starting electric jets. His idea is to have jets that will take off vertically like a helicopter but fly faster than the speed of sound. Of course, it will require many top-level engineers to achieve that engineering feat. But if Elon has proven anything it is this: once he sets his eyes on something, he will get there.

The Musk Foundation

Amid all his crazy schedule, Elon also has a foundation. He started it with his brother in 2001, way before Elon was a household name. Elon is the sole funder and the Foundation has given away millions of dollars to all sorts of causes.

Twitter

Elon Musk is an active Twitter user. He shares his thoughts, concerns, plans and progress on the platform where he has close to 100 million followers. Then one day in 2022, Elon decided to buy Twitter. He said he wants to make Twitter better for everyone.

fact

In early 2007, Robert Downey Jr (RDJ) was preparing to film the first Iron Man. While thinking of an inspiration for Tony Stark which he played, he came across Elon's name. He learnt that Elon had built an industrial complex of his own and he thought it would be a good idea to pay him a visit.

RDJ got a personal tour of the SpaceX headquarters from Elon Musk. RDJ was thoroughly impressed by the scale of SpaceX factory and by Elon. RDJ had expected Elon to be a total geek but what he saw instead was a very motivated person who was willing to roll up his sleeves like any other workers in his factory. And he had a lot of ideas on how Iron Man's power could work. Elon is not quite like Tony Stark but he certainly inspired RDJ to put up a very convincing role as the Iron Man. For Iron Man 2, Elon even made a brief appearance in the film.

As a tribute to Elon, RDJ had a Tesla Roadster placed along with the impressive car collection of Tony Stark during the filming. But it stole the show away from Audi cars. Audi was one of the main sponsors for Iron Man movies. For Iron Man 2, Tesla asked if they can put another of their cars in the movie. Audi said no.

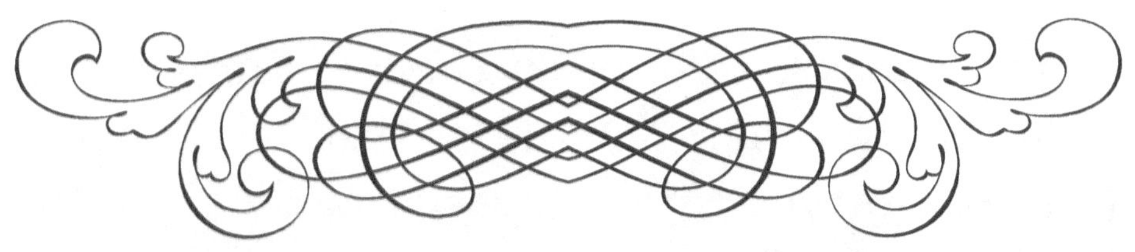

XII. THE VISIONARY

"Truly creative individuals are those who succeed, against all pressures of instinct and worldly wisdom, in visualizing a way of life that will make the lot of others freer and happier." — Mihaly Csikszentimihalyi

In the recorded history of humanity, there has been people who became the hallmark of the times they lived in. They were scientists like

Albert Einstein, inventors like Thomas Edison and artists like Marilyn Monroe and Leonardo da Vinci, people who represented the best in an entire generation, and who in their lifetimes forever changed the course of the world as they knew then. Elon Musk is definitely the person of our times.

Some ideas are so big that their full impact can be felt only generations later. Not everyone in this generation will enjoy the benefits of the revolutions Elon is leading be it electric vehicles, rockets or artificial intelligence. More than the cars and rockets, his biggest impact is on the way we as a human species think about problems and relook at our priorities. For this, Elon is not just an engineer or a businessman. He is a true visionary.

A visionary is someone who is capable of imagining a better future and taking the necessary steps towards that better future. And that future should be better for everyone. When Elon thinks of the future, he thinks of humanity as one. Look, for instance, at his push for electric cars.

When he started the electric car business, his primary concern was not about reversing climate change as result of humans burning carbon. Even though climate change is a concern for the world, there are still doubts if climate change is made worse by burning fossil fuel. Elon's primary concern was that economic progress of the entire world depends on fossil fuel. But the fossil fuels, be it oil, natural gas or coal, are finite. If we keep burning them, they will one day run out completely. Then what?

Without an alternative source of energy, the day we run out of fossil fuel will be a doomsday for humanity. Just imagine if there is not enough oil to run the cars of the world tomorrow – there will be street fights which will soon turn into wars between countries. Only by taking steps to finding an alternative source of energy can we prevent such an event from arising. Elon's solution is to go electric. And since cars and vehicles consume the most fossil fuel, building an electric car powered by renewable energy appeared the most logical to him.

With SpaceX, Elon's vision is bigger, far bigger. In fact, it is so big that there is little chance that it will be realized in his lifetime – to make humans a multi-planetary species. But even here, his logic is crystal clear.

Earth is the only planet with life that we know of. In our galaxy and other billions of galaxies in the universe, there may be other habitable planets like Earth but even if such planets exist, we don't know. What if something terribly bad happens to Earth? Say, like an extinction event that wipes out life from Earth? Such mass extinction events have happened in the past, with the most famous being the asteroid that killed the dinosaurs and eliminated close to ninety percent of life on the planet.

If such an extinction event wipes out the human species, it will be millions of years before another intelligent lifeform evolves, that is provided that Earth still remains intact as a planet sand is not swirling as a cloud of rocks and dust in the space in the millions of years it takes for life to evolve. The present level of human intelligence and technology provide us the necessary resources to start making preparation to avoid such a thing from happening to life. We should have a second home planet, a third and so on. In other words, human should be a multi-planetary, and even multi-galactic species.

Such an idea sounds like the stuff of science fiction. But it is really a person thinking at a superior level. To Romans, landing on the Moon was even beyond fiction. It would have sounded lunatic. But in 1969, two men landed on the moon using nothing but human intelligence. When we think of the new discoveries that will be made in the coming years, the knowledge that will be accumulated, making humans multi-planetary does not really seem impossible. There will be failures, trials and errors, but the there is a probability of success, even if it is small.

Having a clear vision is a necessity. If you are in New York planning to go to London, your vision is to arrive in London. When the vision is clear, and you set about fulfilling it, you find ways. You can take a flight or a boat to reach London. You could swim across to the other side of the pond. There are ways even if someone tells you that you can't reach it.

In a way, humans always function with a goal in mind. Whatever we do, we do to achieve a goal. We just don't drive around and claim we have reached our destination wherever we make the first stop. We first decide on our destination and then start the journey. A vision is simply a grander goal.

But if your vision is not clear, if it is constructed on false beliefs and wrong information, you have no way of realizing your goal. If someone, for instance, told you that London is somewhere in Africa, you can have the fastest jet and you still cannot reach London if you are searching for it in Africa.

The clarity of vision is like the North Star. You may be thrown off course by challenges. The kind of challenge Elon faced all along the way. But he was able to stay true to the course.

There will be people who jeer you, including experts who have no expertise. These include politicians and even your friends. When the first launch of Falcon 1 ended up in an explosion, Elon's friends made a compilation of all the rocket explosions and forced him to watch it. They meant well because they thought Elon was throwing money away by building rockets. But they did not know that Elon's goal was not to save money. It was much bigger.

Even your heroes can turn against you. Elon idolized Neil Armstrong, the first man to land on the Moon. But Neil Armstrong opposed commercial space exploration. It hit Elon particularly hard. He even cried on TV recalling the hurt he felt from his hero's rejection when he was trying to live up to his hero's legacy. He was sad his hero did not encourage him to go for his dreams. But he was even more hurt when Neil Armstrong refused Elon's many invitations to visit SpaceX so that he can show his hero what he has done. Unfortunately, that is not going to happen. Neil Armstrong died in 2012. Even in the face of such hurdles, you can push ahead because you have a clear vision.

A clear vision will guide you away even from

your own devils. People without bigger visions find ways to destroy themselves. Think of rock stars who find fame and money, but their lack of vision takes them on a path of party, drugs and ultimate ruin.

It is possible that our inner devils will come out when we get riches beyond imagination. We want to act rich, important and powerful, and slowly we move away from reality. Instead of working on our vision, we want to enjoy. But this path ultimately leads to self-destruction.

Like all humans, Elon was tempted by the riches he earned. He bought a private jet and multiple homes in posh areas as his popularity grew. He was going the path of vain celebrities. But his vision brought him back to his true path. He sold all his homes, and now stays in a rented house. Like his experiment living on one dollar a day, he sleeps on the couches of his friends when he travels instead of staying in luxury hotels. He spends minimum on buying expensive but useless stuffs. He has his jet only because it takes him places much faster. With his vision, he is able to avoid the many traps that ruin life.

A clear vision becomes a necessity especially for large organizations made up of thousands of workers. When employees believe in a vision, they are able to put in 140 hours a week into their work, and shed tear and blood to achieve it. A janitor who believes in a company's vision is not just cleaning toilets, but, in the case of SpaceX, is trying to colonize Mars.

The ability to have a clear vision and go for it is a form of high intelligence in humans. So, start today. Create a clear vision. And work towards it.

Like all super-rich Americans like Jeff Bezos and Warren Buffet, Elon is often accused of paying very low taxes. By using loopholes that protect the rich, some rich people find ways to avoid taxes while accumulating immense wealth year after year. But Elon is not one of them. In 2021, Elon paid a total of US$ 11 billion in taxes to become the person who paid the highest tax in the entire history of the world. Elon also does not have a house. He rents and sleeps on couches at friends' places when he is travelling. Elon claims that he is not doing what he does for money. And that is true. In June 2014, Elon announced that the hundreds of patents held by Tesla would be free for use to anyone without having to pay Tesla a dime.

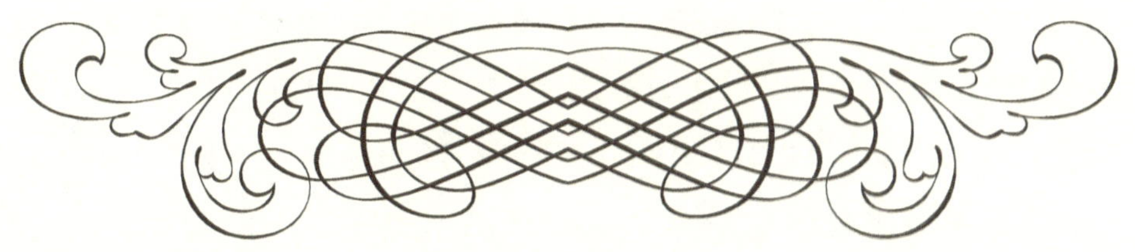

XIII. THE DEFENDER OF FREEDOM

On February 24, 2022, Russia invaded Ukraine. In the lead up to the invasion, Russia amassed hundreds of thousands of troops along the border with Ukraine. A large number of Russian soldiers were also sent to Belarus, Russia's allay to the north of Ukraine. Russia's blatant lies that the militarization of the borders with Ukraine was for a regular military exercise was uncover by

British and American intelligence months in advance but not many countries believed it possible that full scale war would return to Europe after the destructions of the Second World War.

Considered to be the world's second most powerful military, Russia's army invaded Ukraine from multiple fronts. In the early hours of February 24, Russia's precision missiles hit targets across Ukraine knocking out its vital communication infrastructure. In a matter of days, Russian soldiers were in the outskirts of Kyiv, the capital of Ukraine. All odds were against Ukraine and it appeared Ukraine would fall within two weeks, as Moscow had planned.

But Ukraine was prepared to take on the invaders. Although it had a much smaller military and lacked the hardware of Russia, Ukraine had built a formidable defense ever since Russia annexed Crimea in 2014. Already hit hard once by Russia, Ukraine had learnt its lesson and prepared well.

Once Russia's brute force in the early days

weakened due to the poor chain of command, logistical issues and generally a poorly arranged military. Ukraine successfully repealed the invading forces from its capital city and sent the Russians fleeing across to Belarus from where they had come.

The comedian-turned-President of Ukraine used his innate communication skills to inspire his nation to fight back while pleading with world leaders for ammunition and hardware to beat Russians. While arms from the United States, UK and other European countries flowed into Ukraine, what it needed desperately was the restoration of its communication network destroyed completely by Russia. Without secured communication, its smaller military would have had much difficulty taking on Russia.

This is where Elon Musk came to Ukraine's rescue, as if he was destined to defend Ukraine's freedom. Starlink satellite communication systems were easy to transport and set up in the battlefield. Elon Musk donatated more than 20,000 Starlink communication systems to Ukraine at the cost of US$100 million. In a matter of days, Ukraine got its communication systems set up and its military was now on the offensive as Russians retreated.

Of course, Russia was prepared for electronic warfare. It had the technology to block and disrupt satellite communications. It initially did not think Starlink would be a gamechanger in the battlefields of Ukraine. After all, a powerful signal jammer would render the satellite receiver useless. Russia tried but all it took was a few lines of code for Starlink to become immune to Russia's electronic warfare.

With a single decision, Elon Musk emerged as a defender of Ukraine and of the free world.

But Elon's next move was even more daring. In fact, his donation of Starlink systems to Ukraine was peanuts comparing to what he did next. He bought Twitter.

In early 2022, Elon bought a large chunk of Twitter shares. On April 14, 2022, Elon, in response to another Twitter user, said he was going to buy Twitter. Many thought it as nothing more than a joke Elon cracks every once in a while. The only problem was he wasn't joking.

After a bit of back and forth between Elon and Twitter execs – that too through tweets – Elon finally bought the platform for US$44 billion.

Never a person to shy away from more work, Elon fired almost everyone at Twitter including its CEO, stripped it to the bone in terms of employees, and made himself the CEO of Twitter. He set to work, cleaning the platform of bot accounts and making it generally more open to different viewpoints. He even restored the account of Donald Trump which was suspended after he left White House.

When asked why he bought Twitter – a loss-making company – Elon said he wanted to protect freedom of speech. How he turns the company around and make it a platform for free speech is to be seen.

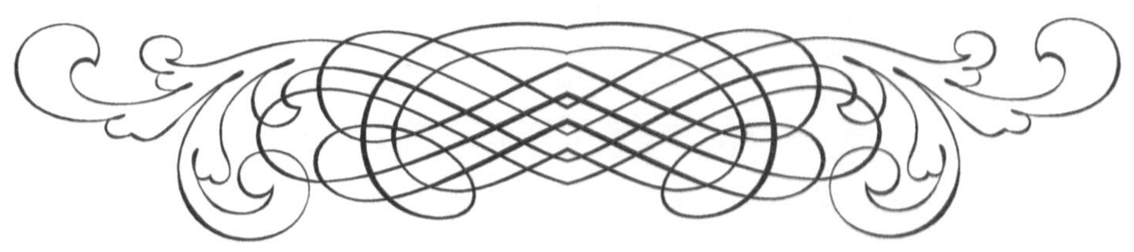

XIV. WORDS OF WISDOM

• I would read everything that I could get my hands on, from when I woke up to when I went to sleep.

• I care a lot about the truth of things and trying to understand the truth of things. I think that's important. If you're going to come up with some solution, then the truth is really, really important.

• I would always think about something, and whether that thing was really true or not and could something else be true, or is there a better conclusion that one could draw that's more probable. I was doing that when I was in elementary school. It would infuriate my parents by the way, that I just wouldn't believe them when they said something, because I would ask them why, then I would consider if that response makes sense given everything else I know.

• If you properly frame the question, the answer is the easy part.

• You should take the approach that you're wrong. Your goal is to be less wrong.

• I think it is possible for ordinary people to choose to be extraordinary.

• It's also very important to teach to the problems and not to the tools. You can imagine like if you say, we want to understand how an internal combustion engine works. The best way to do that is to say let's take apart the engine and put it back together again. Now what tools do we need for this? We need a screwdriver, we need a wrench, maybe a winch, and as you take the engine apart you understand the reason for these tools. If on the other hand you have a course on screwdrivers and a course on wrenches, that would be a terrible way to do it, it's difficult to remember. The way that our mind has evolved is to remember things that are relevant, and to discard information that it thinks has irrelevance, so we must establish relevancy. Tying it to a problem is very powerful for establishing relevance, and getting kids excited about what they're working on, and having the knowledge stick. In the course of solving a problem, taking the engine apart and putting it back together, you learn about the relevance. It's very painful and difficult to remember things if they seem abstract and unimportant. You have to establish the relevancy and importance, and establish the why of things in order for the knowledge to naturally stay in your brain.

• It is important to view knowledge as sort of a semantic tree -- make sure you understand the fundamental principles, i.e. the trunk and big branches, before you get into the leaves and details, or there is nothing for them to hang on to.

• Analogies are very seductive they can sound very compelling, but analogy is just a story. If you want to do something that is fundamentally new or is particularly counterintuitive, then analogies don't work very well.

• I think I'm good at inventing solutions to problems. Things seem fairly obvious to me that are clearly not obvious to most people. And I'm not really trying to do it or anything. It just seems like I see the truth of things and others seem less able to do so.

• Start somewhere and then really be prepared to question your assumptions, fix what you did wrong, and adapt to reality

• Do what you like doing.

• You need to know how the universe works, and you need to know how the economy works.

•	I got some books on how to teach yourself programming and taught myself how to write software. I just started writing software, I really liked computers and programming was fun. I could make my own games, and I also wanted to see how the games worked. Like, how did you create a video game? It was kind of amazing that computers do all those things. You construct a little universe.

•	I don't ever give up.

•	If other people are putting in 40-hour workweeks, and you're putting in 100-hour workweeks, then, even if you're doing the same thing, you will achieve in four months what it takes them a year to achieve.

•	"If he believes it's possible – and he always does when it's a problem he's working on – there's no option for turning back with him. When 99.99 percent of people would have given up, Elon finds the solution that amazes everyone around him" Kimbal

•	I think you have to enjoy what you are doing. Otherwise, it is hard to do it. There are three things you look for. You have to look forward in the morning to doing your work. You do want to have a significant financial reward. And you want to have a possible effect on the world. If you can find all three, you have something you can tell your children.

• We don't think too much about what competitors are doing because I think it's important to be focused on making the best possible products. It's maybe analogous to what they say about if you're in a race: don't worry about what the other runners are doing—just run.

• The biggest mistake in general that I've made—and I'm trying to correct for that—is to put too much of a weighting on somebody's talent and not enough on their personality. . . . It actually matters whether somebody has a good heart. It really does. And I've made the mistake of thinking that sometimes it's just about the brain.

• I think it's incredibly important that you have an environment in general where people look forward to coming to work because it's just so much easier to work hard if you love what you're doing.

• A small group of very technically strong people will always beat a large group of moderately strong people.

• You can learn whatever you need to do to start a successful business either in school or out of school. A school, in theory, should help accelerate that process, and I think oftentimes it does. It can be an efficient learning process, perhaps more efficient than empirically learning lessons. There are examples of successful entrepreneurs who never graduated high school, and there are those that have PhDs. I think the important principle is to be dedicated to learning what you need to know, whether that is in school or empirically.

• I am a volunteer. I don't need the money.

• When we started Tesla, our chance of success was 10%.

• If we think it's worth buying life insurance on an individual level, then perhaps it's worth spending something on life insurance for life as we know it, and arguably that expenditure should be greater than zero.

•	When something is important enough, you do it even if the odds are not in your favor.

•	The first step is to establish that something is possible; then probability will occur.

•	You must be willing to lose it all, but be willing to keep going into the future.

•	Failure is a good option. If you are not failing, you are not trying hard enough.

•	Pay attention to negative feedback, and solicit it, particularly from friends.

•	People should pursue what they are passionate about. That will make them happier than pretty much anything else.

•	It is OK to have your eggs in a basket as long as you control what happens to that basket.

• I think that is the single best piece of advice: constantly think about how you could be doing things better and questioning yourself.

• Some people don't like change, but you need to embrace change if the alternative is disaster.

• Don't tell me what you like; tell me what you don't like.

• People work better when they know what the goal is and why. It is important that people look forward to coming to work in the morning and enjoy working.

• I think we have a duty to maintain the light of consciousness to make sure it continues into the future.

• Don't confuse schooling with education. I didn't go to Harvard but the people that work for me did.

•   I could either watch it happen or be a part
of it.

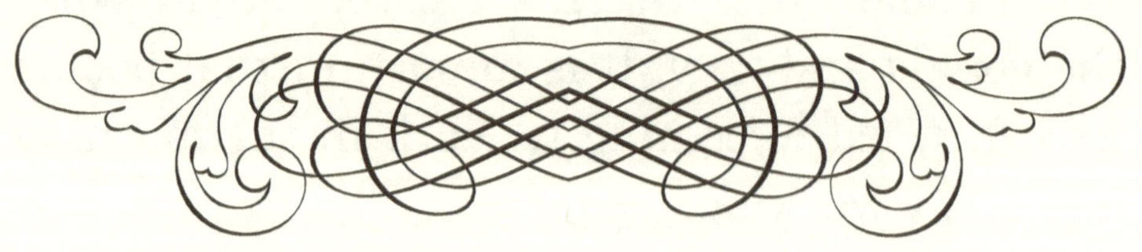

* 9 7 9 8 2 2 3 7 0 0 9 2 0 *